BLINDSIDED
Has the Old Man Bewitched You?

Freshwater Press

USA

All Scripture references taken from the KJV of the Holy Bible, unless otherwise indicated.

BLINDSIDED: *Has the Old Man Bewitched You?*
Freshwater Press
USA

ISBN: 978-1-960150-13-4
Paperback version

Copyright 2022 by Dr. Marlene Miles
All rights reserved.

Contents

5 ___ Blindsided

11 ___ Your Scroll

15 ___ Stupid Sin

21 ___ Wake Up

26 ___ Has A Curse Landed?

31 ___ Shh! It's a Secret

35 ___ Satan Cannot Cast Our Satan

37 ___ Fairytales

40 ___ The Boyfriend

46 ___ The Old Man

55 ___ Designs on You

57 ___ Collateral Damage

60 ___ What's Wrong With These Guys?

62 ___ The Professional Guy

72 ___ This Not His Real Life

75 ___ This Is Not Your Life

79 ___ Don't Accept Them

82 ___ Don't Get Used to It

84 ___ Discernment Off

89 ___ Unwilling to Recognize A Demon

90___Recognize God

92___Over You

95___Multiple Bewitchments

97___It's Compounding

101__Prayer Covering

103__See To It Yourself

106__Then the Prayers Start

110__What Kind of King?

117___*Christian Books by this Author*

119___*Journals and Devotionals by this Author*

120___*Illustrated Children's Books by this Author*

Blindsided

> O foolish Galatians, who hath bewitched you, that ye should not obey the truth, before whose eyes Jesus Christ hath been evidently set forth, crucified among you?
>
> Galatians 3:1

Can you imagine getting far along into your life, or far along in adulthood, to finally realize that you haven't lived life on your own terms at all, but that you've been living a counterfeit life? A **bewitched life**? Not the kind of bewitched as in the movies or on TV whereby wiggling your nose or nodding your head suddenly everything works in your favor, but the kind of life where the occult is really *occult* to you. *Occult,* meaning *hidden.*

You have no idea that there are or have been things working to sway you into or away from certain things, places, situations, and some of those situations were to be to your advantage and for your success in life. There was evil spiritual manipulation, control or domination over you and your life's choices.

There are things in your life that you did not give approval to, but you were subjected to—, things *not* of God.

Perhaps very late in life you find out that you've been bewitched, and you've been or are operating your life according to someone else's will, not your own. How have people exerted sway or force over you without your knowledge or approval?

Witchcraft.

Worst of all, what if you found that you've been operating your whole life based on the whims of *demons* and not what you actually want?

Can you imagine **never** finding out any of this until you get to Glory, past the Pearly Gates, when the Lord Jesus Christ Himself or an *intake* Angel asks you what were you doing on Earth for the past 100 years? Why didn't you have **control** of and control over your own life?

You may swear (don't swear) ... you may seriously believe that you did have control and you have lived according to the Word of God and by your own free will. *Oh really?*

Did you take the right career course? If so, why did you complain about your job so often? Did you marry the right spouse? If so, why did it turn out the way it did?

Did you have the kids you were supposed to have? You need the right spouse to have had the right children.

Did you fulfill the Ministry and Kingdom work that GOD gave you to fulfill?

Or are the answers to all those questions, *Sort of. Kind of. Possibly, I don't know,* or *I did the best that I could.*

Did you meet the right people in your life that you were supposed to meet? Did you have the right relationships with those right people? Or did you suffer wrong destiny connections? Did you meet and have relationships with counterfeit people you were never supposed to meet or interact with?

Did you meet **more enemies** than friends? Was there trouble all the time? Something to solve every week, or every day?

Something to figure out? something to get away from, or correct?

None of those situations would be God's best for you, would it? Surely God did not set you on Earth to afflict you. All of this drama and trauma would be clues that things are wrong if you were discerning.

Did you meet divine helpers? Destiny helpers? Or does it/did it seem that everyone you met **competed against you** and never really _helped_ you--, even family members? *Especially family members?*

Is this possible? And if it is, how?

Shakespeare said that the whole world is a stage and each person, is an actor playing their part. Who writes the Script to your life? Who writes the Script to anyone's life? Too many worry that **God** will tell them what to do or that God demands certain behavior and action from them. Too many run *from* God just in case they want to do something that God does not want them to do. Or they may run from God in case God is about to tell them to do something they do not want to do. Too many run from God as if God has a script and a part that they just do not want to play out.

Without God it is impossible <u>not</u> to live a bewitched life if someone is determined to bewitch you, and you are susceptible to witchcraft.

NOT "BELIEVING" IN WITCHCRAFT DOES NOT GET YOU OFF THE HOOK OF BEING BEWITCHED. As a matter of fact, the more you do *not* believe in witchcraft the easier of a target you are.

Your Scroll

God has a scroll for your life. He has a scroll for each of our lives and He is the only one who knows in full what that scroll reads. Now you may say that you don't believe in predestination.

> For we are his workmanship, created in Christ Jesus unto good works, which God hath before ordained that we should walk in them.
>
> Ephesians 2:10

Millenia ago, darkness hovered over the face of the deep. Once God set order there was order. There is no way that you can think that God just threw you here on Earth and said, *"There you go, do whatever you want to do."* While at the same time we have free will, God's outcome(s) will prevail, God just gives us the opportunity to get where we are supposed to go the slow, arduous, painful way, or His way, the Righteous Way.

Further, regarding all mankind, God has a complete plan for man; the part you play can be completed by you or you can fail miserably by choice, disobedience, or in ignorance being derailed, re-directed and missing the mark completely. In that case, God will get someone else to complete the part of **His Plan** that you failed to execute.

> Yet I have left *me* seven thousand in Israel, all the knees which have not bowed unto Baal, and every mouth which hath not kissed him.
>
> 1 Kings 19:18

Saint of God, you may be your momma's or your daddy's only child, but you are not God's *only*. If you want success in God, seek His face and His plan for your purpose, your life and your ministry. Else, those who wish to break you down, tear you down, tear you to shreds may have access to you.

I come in the volume of the book where it is written about me and so do you (Psalm 40:7). The volume of the Book where it is written about you IS your Scroll; it is the Lord's scroll for your life. It is blueprint for the successful life with an expected end, Amen. (Jeremiah 29:11).

> Then said I, Lo, I come (in the volume of the book it is written of me,) to do thy will, O God. Hebrews 10:7

God has a volume, a scroll regarding your life--, the timing of it, when you were born, what things you will do, what gifts you have and resources you will have to work the part of the Great Commission that God has for the full redemption of mankind.

And you know that's true. One of the ways man gets into so much trouble and one of the ways he opens up demonic doors is trying to know the future. How does he do that? Usually by witchcraft, soothsayers, diviners. Man regards astrologers, shamans, witch doctors, voodoo priests and the like, while trying to know the future, get out of trouble, get money, wealth or fame, find love or undo someone else who already has any or all of those things.

The one person who has all of those answers and will also tell them to you for FREE is God, Jesus Christ, by His Holy Spirit. Just pray and ask Him and He will reveal Himself. He will reveal all Truth. He will reveal secrets. He will reveal riches (true riches), and His love and peace to you.

Stupid Sin

They say sin makes you stupid. The Bible says it a nicer way. It says that our senses are *dulled* after sin. I'd say our senses are dulled also before sin; else we couldn't be so easily lulled **into sin**. So *stupid* and dullness starts before or at, and after sin until confession, repentance, man becomes *stuck on sin, stuck on stupid*, and that's a real SOS.

> They are darkened in their understanding and separated from the life of God because of the ignorance that is in them due to the hardening of their hearts. Having lost all sensitivity, they have given themselves over to sensuality so as to indulge in every kind of impurity and they are full of greed. Ephesians 4:18-19

Sin obscures and blinds a man's mind so that man misses the obvious and of course cannot see that themselves are sinful, since all the ways of a man are clean in his own eyes. Witchcraft can blind the mind, even the eyes and ears of a victim, temporarily or sometimes even longer. Witchcraft (wizardry) can make the room stand still, while a man does something illegal right in front of his wife, and others but they never see it. NONE of them. I saw it, no one else did.

I've been at a dinner party where this old man, whom I will now call the wizard said, to me, *I would like **you** to pass me the salt, only you.* As soon as he said it everyone at the table got up, in tandem, left the room as if they had an important meeting in the ladies room or somewhere. I passed the salt and as soon as I did, all the dinner guests just came back into the room as suddenly as they had left, as if they had just taken a brisk walk around the block. This whole thing took about a minute and a half and there were four or five people who went into the bedroom or a single bathroom in a single woman's apartment. Not only did they leave the room, they shut the door to the room they went to. It was really odd. Did they know the salt had been moved? Did they care? Was it important? No. BUT WE ALL WERE STILL IN THE MIDDLE OF THE MEAL.

The chandelier might have started talking right then, because I was ready to get out of there. But I didn't know how to do that gracefully.

You too, have been in a room where this has happened, that is if you have ever been to a magic show. If you haven't been to a magic show but you've seen it on television, it is the same principle and you have participated in it or been a victim to it. It's as though your mind, eyes, ears, understanding is **<u>suspended</u>** briefly, quickly, unbeknownst to you while the "magician" does his "*trick.*" Being in the presence of this "magic" opens you up for more demonic activity. So, stay away from it.

A darkened or dulled mind does not lend itself to intelligence; it makes one stupid or more stupid if he keeps sinning, especially repeating the same sin.

The stupidity of sinning and believing he can continue sinning, or simply **stop** sinning when he gets ready is not smart. I can stop smoking, drinking, overeating, lazing on the couch, vaping ____ (you fill in the blank), anytime I want to. To stop sinning takes **power**. If a man thinks he can just <u>stop</u> sinning and pretend he never sinned as if to say, "*Never mind,*" he is mistaken. The repercussion of that sin is still there. Time does not heal unrepented of sin.

Deliverance from sin and the repercussions of it takes repentance and Jesus Christ. It takes power. It takes *will power* yes, but it takes a *spiritual* **power** that a sinner does not have either because the power that caused him to sin is already greater than he was, OR the sin itself zapped the spiritual prowess that the man originally had. And in so doing – he falls into sin.

He falls.

It takes power to stand. It takes power to withstand. It takes power to stand therefore, without power; man falls.

There's Adam and Eve standing right where they sinned, hiding—*trying* to hide. You can hide from a dead idol; it will NEVER find you. You can hide from the Elf on the Shelf, but how can you hide from God? Moreover, how can you hide *sin* from God?

Although God hates sin and doesn't look on it, He **knows**. The stench of sin is worse than the funkiest dumpster, cesspool, sewage, or garbage heap you'd ever smell. Even if you think you could hide from the visibility of God, how do you think you'd cover that **smell**?

He knows.

Wake Up

In your life you never planned to sin, right? You never wanted to sin--, but you did. Then one day you wake up to the possibility or the reality that strange things are happening or have happened to you, so you finally start looking around and not just in the mirror to adjust the appearance of your carnal man and your outside face for the people that you will encounter at work, on the train, and at your social settings. You finally start looking around to see what has happened to your life? What has happened *in* your life and does your environment have anything to do with it?

Not that you are shirking responsibility or casting blame on anything or anyone, but as many of us may have felt, you may feel, ***I have not done ANYTHING to deserve how my life is going right now.*** I've noticed that ever since this or that happened, things have been different and not in a good way... You begin to see patterns.

Stay with that line of thinking, it will get you somewhere.

Still, there is sin. Sin, and its wages. The wages of sin are death. Death of something, usually the death of something desirable, something you like or want, but it dies. A career. A marriage. A family. A life???

Dullness and sin may make a man continue to sin.

Therefore to him who knows to do good and does not do it, to him it is sin. James 4:17 NKJV

> I do not understand what I do. For what I want to do I do not do, but what I hate I do. ¹⁶ And if I do what I do not want to do, I agree that the law is good. ¹⁷ As it is, it is no longer I myself who do it, but it is sin living in me. Romans 7:15-17

Jesus didn't have any witchcraft worked on Him; He truthfully said, the devil has nothing in Him. Once we sin, we become susceptible to devilish plots and schemes. We all have sinned and fallen short of the Glory of God; therefore, sin, witchcraft, curses, spells can alight. It's part of the Curse of the Law. God said in Deuteronomy if you do this or don't do that (sins) then these things can come upon you. Yeah, there is bad stuff waiting to come upon you.

There you are living your comfortable life in your comfortable house on your comfortable sofa. Evil knocks at the door, it's

SIN. Your butler gets up, goes to the door and throws it open wide for all that evil. Lord, help us all.

If we need tender mercies every morning from God, if we need to forgive others as we are also forgiven, if we need to forgive 70 X 7, then that's a whole lot of sin. All day? Even at night when we sleep, our spirit man is doing what? Possibly sinning. The devil's goal is to defile us, so the perfect time to attempt it is when our minds (and bodies) are resting, and our spirit man is running the show.

Who is your spirit man? Can your spirit man handle the spiritual assaults the devil throws your way, especially when your conscious mind is not in the game because you are asleep?

Witchcraft works by throwing some assault your way. It sends you into a trauma and tizzy if possible. There are flesh and soul responses which set off a cascade of more stress, anxiety, worry and if you don't get quick spiritual help, you can spiral downward yourself, doing the rest of the witch or wizard's job for them.

Has A Curse Landed?

Something strange is happening or has happened. Just as public service announcements implore listeners to know the signs of any dread natural disease, such as heart attack, stroke, diabetes – I am urging Christians to KNOW THE SIGNS OF WITCHCRAFT attack. I won't cite them yet, but when you get to chapter called The Professional Guy, you will see them clearly.

Not only that, some of these strange things that happened to you had narration (like an evil movie villain, if you happened to have been listening. This is why it does not behoove one to be tipsy or drunk out of their skull. Evil people tell on themselves all the time if you will but listen. They sometimes may approach another person by asking *you* this, that or the other has happened to you. Sometimes they want to hear your woes to know if their curses hit. If you're suffering or making mistakes in your life that either are devastating to you now or will be devastating in the future, they are really happy. It's about all they can do to keep from laughing out loud or bragging of their evil works.

If you think about it, that is if you can, if your brain is not in a fog, there were signs, and or words that you most often ignored, but culprits, like bad characters in a Scooby Doo movie told on themselves. It was all they could do not to gloat, but there were patterns and *clues*. There were signs. There were phrases uttered, and words spoken.

The time that former co-worker laughed and said, *"Oh, you had a fall,"* and for some reason that was so funny to him. But you hadn't had a fall. In the natural.

Not yet.

Weeks or years later, that time when you turned around in a room and there was nothing to fall over, but you actually fell, and it was as though it was in slow motion. Nothing hurt, you landed softly even and wondered how did I fall? How did I even fall, you ask yourself again. *What* did I stumble on? You didn't stumble, you weren't even walking. You simply **fell** when you turned about to leave the room. You weren't embarrassed because there was no one there. So you thought. Still, in your spirit you knew that God was there, the Holy Spirit or some ministering angel, else that fall could have been very painful and even devastating because it was a very hard tile floor. But you were unhurt.

Physically.

But what else was there? Possibly unseen evil, sent by messengers of evil; harbingers of jealousy and hate. Then you realized that former co-worker wasspeaking the language of witches – something you knew nothing about.

It never occurred to you that someone would laugh when or if someone had a fall. And what did that fellow mean? That fellow that had been terminated from the job because of poor performance and was hurt and/or bitter toward anyone who still worked there, or anyone who he thought was responsible for his being let go, when it was his responsibility to do a good job on his job.

This is how bewitchment works. You think nothing of what could be everyday occurrences. You think no one notices; you barely notice, but something happened and it happened to *you*. You played it out as if on a stage, confirming to the evil agent who sent bewitchment to you that what they desired to happen, *happened*.

Shh! It's A Secret

Here's the unfunny thing about witchcraft, a curse is released, a spell is cast, you know nothing of it. You don't even **believe** that it's a real thing because as soon as you were born your parents and caregivers started **lying** to you may be without even realizing it. They started lying to you so you would have a nice childhood, a fun childhood, full of wonder and imagination.

I know they lied because if they hadn't, you'd have no idea about spells, curses and witchcraft and you'd have no opinion on it because you never would have heard anything about it. But as soon as you are about to go to sleep your first day, week, month or year or life, the lies start. The indoctrination starts. The propaganda starts. Satan's program of lying to children, tell them over and over until they believe it, are so confused that they don't know what to believe. That there are books and books on witches, wizards, evil, elves, leprechauns, faeries, goblins and a host of other entities, **but they don't exist**. And these fairy tales are all about magic, but magic doesn't exist either. But there are magicians who entertain grown people, but magic doesn't exist.

Which is it? Really?

So you **have** made a decision on whether these things exist or not because you have been made to believe that they do not exist. You've closed your mind to their existence, well I mean the saved people. You're too intelligent to believe (in) that.

Yet, there are plenty who practice the dark arts, more than a million in the USA alone according to current data. And those who believe in something real are not dumber than those who do not believe in something that is real. So why are there so many books written about them? Why is talk of wizards, witches, familiar spirits, soothsayers, diviners, et cetera all through the Bible?

So you, smarty pants believe you know it all because all these lies began with a lie. That lie being, **"Once upon a time."**

To further drive the point home, all the spells, curses, witches and wizards books have *happily-ever-after's* that come after doing little or nothing, so in your adult life you feel you have to do nothing to rectify **real** problems. Or the happy ending comes as a result of magic – *more* magic. Make a wish. Make a wish on *what?* Genies, wizards, magic fish, amulets, potions, rings ... Magic, of course is what cast the curse or spell in the first place.

Satan Cannot Cast Out Satan

Satan cannot cast out Satan so if magic *caused* the problem, more magic won't and can't fix it, it will only make it worse and make your problems worse. Only God. In real life, only God can fix this.

And if Satan cast out Satan, he is divided against himself; how shall then his kingdom stand?
Matt 12:26

Some think themselves lucky to have had a parent to read them bedtime stories. Some learn later that luck is not of God, so those indoctrinating, propaganda-laced, hair-raising stories that lied and lied to a child until they were forced to believe the lie or rebel against it completely may have been more fortunate **not** to have been beat over the head with fairytales and nursery rhymes that confused what could have been a very good developing mind.

So when you run into trouble, no course from the realms of darkness will correct your problem. They may *suspend* it for a while. They may **hide** it for you, for a while, because hiding works on man, even though it doesn't work on God. The game, Peek-a-Boo confuses pretty much every kid and some adults, too.

You can't hide anything from God. But God may be wondering why you are wandering around in darkness trying to find Light.

God may wonder why you are wandering in darkness trying to hide or to be hidden--. Jesus is the Light of the World; you should be reaching out to Him and not more darkness. But first you have to know what darkness is:

Paganism. New Ageism. Wicca and any other forms of witchcraft. Catholicism and other false religions--, voodoo, sangoma, Santeria, magic, black arts, …. As satisfying as it would be to watch evil fight evil, none of those mediums will get you out of a problem that is caused by anyone of those mediums. It will only get you deeper in.

Unless you are fully reprobate God won't bring these problems on you, so pretty much any problem you could be experiencing is brought on by the realms of darkness.

Yes, I'm saying Jesus is the only way out of whatever pit you've been cast into, or caged in, even if you, yourself jumped into that pit.

Fairytales

After telling the lying fairy tales with the lying happily-ever-after lie, the parent then tells the child, *it's not true*. There are no witches, there are no warlocks, there are no wizards. There are no curses or spells. No one can do anything to you, and everything is going to be alright. (Go to sleep and forget about it.)

(Then why waste time telling such a story?) And all of these lies come at night right before the child is to go to sleep. Then the parent tells the child that they love him/her.

No wonder relationships are hard when folks grow up and start to date. There you are, chatting it up on the phone, he tells you some lies – you're used to lies --, especially at night, so your discernment doesn't kick in. Then he tells you he loves you. Okay, standard fare. Your parents did that to you your entire childhood.

You each say goodnight. But you go to sleep and have horrible dreams.

You wake up in the morning and wonder what's wrong with **<u>YOU</u>** because you should be happier than you are. Historically there should have been a happily ever after the lies he told you, plus he said, *I love you* before you went to bed. AT least that's what happened in all the fairytales and most of the books that were read to you as a child.

The Boyfriend

But now you have the relationship with the boy – oh goodie!

Really?

Your best girlfriend, or your own relative for that matter does not approve and they want to break you two up. Maybe they talked to you about it, but it doesn't register to you how intent they are against this relationship.

Maybe they say nothing about it but take matters into their own hands. Perhaps they don't even know that the words they speak have weight. They may begin wishing, believing, muttering, murmuring, talking to anyone who will listen how they want to break you two up – or you two shouldn't be together … too young… or whatever reason. Maybe she likes the boy and wants him to be *her* boyfriend.

Blind witch? Witchcraft runs in the family, but no one knows it yet.

Years ago, my then-stepson took "air scissors" and told me he was cutting the cord between me and his father. His father and I were never even civil to each other since. Where did the kid learn that? TV? Movies? His father? His mother? Is it just in his bloodline?

Something happened in the spirit when the boy did this; no one corrected him, so this thing came to pass--, a 7-year-old kid.

> This is what the Lord commands: When a man makes a vow to the Lord or takes an oath to obligate himself by a pledge, he must not break his word but must do everything he said.

> When a young woman still living in her father's household makes a vow to the LORD or obligates herself by a pledge and her father hears about her vow or pledge but says nothing to her, then all her vows and every pledge by which she obligated herself will stand. But if her father forbids her when he hears about it, none of her vows or the pledges by which she obligated herself will stand; the LORD will release her because her father has forbidden her. Numbers 30:2-5

Teach your kids—male and female children. Watch your kids. Listen to your kids. Correct your kids. Parents are careful that legs aren't broken, bike wreck boo-boo's are mended, bad food is not eaten. WHO is protecting your kids *spiritually*? Who is keeping your child safe *spiritually*? The **Now I Lay Me Down to Sleep** Prayer? That's not enough.

Who is your child, anyway? What Earth assignments does he have from God? What interferences does he have, or might he have from the other side that wants him to fail miserably--, that wants his soul? Fear him who can kill the soul and the body in hell, (Matthew 10:28).

Who's watching and listening to your child, *spiritually t*o keep him out of danger today, tomorrow or even in his future? Most things are easier to deal with if they never come to pass in a person's life.

Think of your own childhood, Ouija Boards, 8 Balls, what other divination games did you play that you thought were innocent then, but you know better now? What are things that you did as a kid that you wouldn't **think** of doing again? Doors may have been opened that still need to be closed in your life. And, if those troubles are in your life, or your spouse's life then it's already in your child's life. Understand that a child could be adding open doors that should never be opened.

Sometimes those doors are opened at the suggestion or urging of childhood friends and playmates who have their own spiritual bent from their own households that you probably know nothing about.

I recall most of the **exciting** suggestions in my childhood came from a relative whom I was relegated to play with. We all thought she was creative – nope, that's not how I would describe it now that I'm grown up and can see better, spiritually. Most of her suggestions were dark and let's face it – WRONG! Where did she even *get* these ideas? Back in that day, in the country, in rural America, we were all watching the same three TV Channels. Where did my relative get these ideas? What other *channels* did she have access to?

I don't know if it's true for many, most, or all, but the excitement of doing something new was most often when that "new" thing was taboo, dangerous, forbidden, or we had to sneak to do it, and then pretty much lie to cover it up. Honestly, I don't think those were my plans as a kid, but I let myself be talked into things far too many times.

Doors. What doors did I open?

Lord, help us all.

The Old Man

So *they* don't approve of the boyfriend or of the relationship? Maybe your parent doesn't want you to date just yet--, or ever. They could be afraid that you will get pregnant and embarrass *them*. Or they don't ever want you to leave home because selfishly they had you to take care of them in their old age.

Folks have motives and you have to dwell with all people according to knowledge. Yes, what you know about them, and what you see them do or not do, but according to knowledge means the knowledge and the Wisdom of God. Things that a person may try to hide are never hidden to God and God can reveal things that seem hidden to you so you can govern yourself accordingly.

It may not be a parent or a relative who is scheming against you, your success in life, or your relationships. It could be a perfect or an imperfect stranger. **It could even be someone you meet at church.**

In my mid to late twenties, I met what should have been a godly, old man at a church conference. He had a whole wife and kids, but he lusted after me all of my adult life, but I never knew it until recently. It took me until **<u>this year</u>** to put it together that every male that he *ever* knew about that I dated as soon as he knew anything about any of them, within hours or days (it rarely took as long as weeks) that male would suddenly stop talking to me. There would be no hard feelings, but the relationship would suddenly fade to black.

This old man still thinks I don't know of his nefarious activities, unless some *familiar* or *monitoring spirit* has revealed to him that I know, and that I've finally figured it out.

How has he interfered in my interpersonal relationships from another entire state, all these years? Is he a wizard? At least. That's not what he calls himself of course, and that is not what people call him; he is or was, held in high esteem by folks.

This old man has people doing his bidding, obviously. He keeps a bevy of young women, many with *familiar spirits* on the line, in the queue for his own personal reasons, I'm sure. And they stay because of whatever counterfeit promise he has made them. I'm not sure if he pretends to be speaking into their lives, helping them or what. Intermittently through my life he has seemed to be a great support. He exhorts easily, but it was only recently I realized how rehearsed his words are, giving the same word to multiple people on different occasions, like a horoscope. (Horror-scope). Over the years he has intimated that he would *rescue* me from relationships that he deems wrong or inappropriate for me--, active relationships that I did not ask to be rescued from

He has promised me positions, titles, notoriety and/or fame that I also have never asked for (or accepted). I have not asked this man for anything or any of this. He came on like tons of bricks as a *friend*. Wanting to believe the fairy tale, I thought wow, a male who only wants to be my friend; how appropriate! But really, he suddenly inserted himself in my life as my friend. I didn't ask for that either.

As Jesus said that the devil had nothing in him. This old man has not yet found what thing that could tempt me, and he will not find it. You know, the thing that makes a person go all goo-gah and become putty in the hands of a manipulating me-too type perpetrator who wants Lord knows from you. I'm sure it's very distressing to him.

So, these other young women – and they are almost exclusively women or young good-looking couples with money flock to him, and he brags about their flocking to him.

You may think this old man wants to **recruit** young women to sleep with. No, that's not it. It's far more sinister than that. It seems he wants to recruit them **by** sleeping with them. Sex is not really what he's looking for, that is a means to an end – what end, I'm not really sure, but I have my suspicions.

Primarily, I believe he is a thief; he came to steal. Steal what? Money? Stars? Gifts. Skills? Abilities? Destiny? Probably all of or some combination of that. But he kept asking me for money and things of monetary value. While at the same time he declared himself a mega millionaire. Why would he ever ask me for any money? That it just all did not add up is enough for this book. I have so much more to tell about this and may put it in another volume with a lot more details.

Does his wife know? Most often I think she does. Well, after I finally got past the part where I believed she was about to die and he was doing things decent and in order, looking for a new wife—with her blessing---, what? Yeah.... That was not the case or the truth, but somehow, she either cares absolutely nothing about this guy right now, or she's in on whatever his schemes are.

This old man does the strangest things, leaves his wife for days and weeks at a time and she doesn't seem to bat an eye. It's probably as sinister as I think, maybe more so. I think she's in on it.

The LORD showed me the two of them in a dream – she was *boiling* spaghetti in the sauce in a big pot. No one boils the spaghetti **in** the sauce. In the dream, I told her the spaghetti was ready, but it was boiling. She said she liked it that way and left the boiling pot, as he came into the house and kitchen (in the dream). Secreted in his hand were three smallish, green, obelisk shaped crystals that he only wanted to show to *me*. She quietly left the kitchen in the dream; the same thing she does in real life like an obedient or bewitched pet.

This bewitchment against me may have been happening through him for **more than 20 years**! Three or four relationships and marriages (of mine) were devastated and broken completely. Am I blaming the old man?

I am blaming the *witchcraft* and if he is the source of this sorcery; yes, I am blaming him. Leading up to me putting this all together we had restored contact after many years – more than a decade. Soon after he got to the point of being verbally angry (abusive in my opinion) with me over *any* male that I know or may talk to or date. Even people that he knew that I was just meeting and have cordial conversations with sent him into a jealous rage. What! I'm not his child and not of the age to be his child. I'm not his wife and obviously the one he has isn't planning to check out.

His children? Yes, all girls, each nearly twice the age to be married. No prospects in sight; he becomes furious if the girls talk about meeting someone or getting married. He thinks he's not obvious. Let him (or her) with spiritual vision see what is happening in the Spirit; Thank you, Lord. He doesn't want any of them to marry; I'm not sure they realize it, but I could see it and hear it.

If anyone comes at me because of this book, it will be him, and then you will know who he is. He might choose to identify himself; I doubt it. Either way; I'm ready because all this is true, and I am authorized of the Lord to write it at this time.

(There is a Part 2 to this, I will call it, **This Old Man**. Look for its release soon.)

Designs on You

There could be people in your life that you know and trust, who may not be related to you at all, but they have their own desires and designs on **YOUR life—the life GOD gave <u>you</u>. You might n**ever suspect them because they are upstanding citizens, and my God, *who thinks like that?*

I suppose those who heard fairytales and *identified with* the witch, the wizard or the villain think like *that.* While we heard the same fairytales and identified with the prince, the princess, the king, the queen, or the damsel in distress.

They may be people of position and authority. Many times that's who can afford to enter into secret societies or pay someone to direct evil at people that they consider enemies, competition, or objects of affection. Some of them are pastors and leaders in the Church which is the perfect cover to do evil against a perceived nemesis or a romantic interest, on the low.

Walk circumspectly. That's what the Bible says. Be gentle as doves and wise as serpents.

> See then that ye walk circumspectly,
> not as fools, but as wise,
> Ephesians 5:15

Collateral Damage

Listen closely: sometimes there could be absolutely no one after you, but somehow you may be unknowingly *interfering* in an evil person's plans against someone else's life. While doing so, if you are in a dry season of prayer yourself, or worse, in active sin you will be very susceptible to any Curse of the Law.

Under the Curse of the Law, understand that when we sin it is **LEGAL** for a curse to come upon us. And how do curses come? Someone sends them. Either actively like an erupting volcano or storm that is right now. Or curses could have been established down your family line hundreds and hundreds of years ago and perpetuated. The ground of your life and your bloodline rumbles from time to time then a seismic event, a *cursequake (my word)* rattles and shakes your foundation because of bloodline curses that ARE **allowed** because of past sin, ancestral sin and evil covenants, unrepented for sin, un-renounced dedications and also current sin.

If you sin, you are susceptible. It's as though sin puts a magnet on you and evil comes to latch on to that magnet.

Evil that could be happening to you or may have already happened to you may be because you were in *association* with someone who was receiving evil arrows and they didn't know it, either. That makes anything that happens to you **collateral damage**.

Come out from among them…

Wherefore come out from among them, and be ye separate, saith the Lord, and touch not the unclean thing; and I will receive you.

2 Corinthians 6:17

Don't sit in the counsel of the ungodly, don't hang out with evil people. An obvious sinner is wide open to all sorts of evil. Physical evil, spiritual evil, it is far too dangerous.

So we know what the Bible says – at least some of it. We know what we were taught in Sunday School as children. I guess the answer is: Go ahead and live a while then you will see WHY God said this in His Word. Why God said that--, it's so this stuff that seems to be coming upon you, doesn't.

What's Wrong With These Guys?

In my romantic and marriage life I've been left for decades to wonder first, what's wrong with *me*? Then, once I became wiser, I'd wonder **what's wrong with these guys?**

Let's answer that in two parts, second part first, the guys: Either their own ancestral foundations and/or current local or environmental witchcraft, such as that Old Man who we have discussed, is what's wrong with these guys. If curses are sent to a person that another person is associated with, that can very well affect all parties involved.

For example, if someone sends a poverty curse and it hits, the person hit may then borrow money from a friend or relative. Now that person is in **agreement** with the cursed person, putting money on the cursed person's *altar*, which is jacked up right now with sin. They just bought into that drama.

If a person is under judgment from God, do not interfere. *(That's another whole book.)*

Quick Questionnaire:

1. Is your husband/wife or significant someone under witchcraft attack?
2. Can they see it?
3. Are they willing to do anything about it?
4. Or are they planning to stay broken and break your life in the process?

The Professional Guy

I'll come back to me in a minute, but I want to tell you a real story of the professional guy. His *sister* (and possibly mother—she learned it somewhere), has put witchcraft on her brother for years. She seems torn as to whether to like his profession and how much money he makes or to be jealous of it; it's obvious she wants it. She doesn't work, and pretty much never has. This woman will ask her brother for $2.00 if they are out anywhere. $2.00! (she's 45+ years old.)

Their mother, on her deathbed assigned the son to take care of his sister, five years his junior. Even though the sister had her own husband at the time, she thinks her brother should provide for the lifestyle that she *wants* which is far and away better than what her real husband could ever afford. So, like another bad episode of Scooby Doo she uses black arts to drive off anyone that her brother could be interested in romantically, seriously--, *financially*.

I asked him how much his sister had to do with the breakup of his marriage of 15 years – his silence and sudden head jerk toward me let me know that he knew, but he was surprised that I knew.

Pray: God will always show you things if you pray.

Very recently as the Professional Guy had become single, he was interested in a **_young_** woman. I don't know if it was reciprocated or not, but shortly after he was single and able to approach her, that **_young_** woman was suddenly **dead** under mysterious circumstances. We can't go into the details of it right now because it is just too ID Discovery for this book.

This professional man exhibits **all** the signs of witchcraft attack. **ALL OF THEM**. He is the perfect candidate because he will emphatically state, *"I don't believe in any of that stuff."*

He's awkward. He's unsteady. He has fallen at least twice in the parking lot at work. Sometimes he has to lean just to stay vertical. He gets vertigo at random times. He has phantom pains; he gets things checked out medically, but nothing is ever wrong with him. He can't sleep. He can't go to sleep easily. He can't stay asleep. He prescription dopes to fall asleep but that doesn't always work. He is an ungodly man and wakes up cussing because he's exhausted every morning. He has severe headaches any day of the week. His hands shake with intention tremor which inhibits him from doing his professional job. He experienced a severe hand burn one day when cooking and lost all confidence in the kitchen. That also affected his work for more than a week. He has had to downgrade his profession just to work at all. He's in a brain fog most of the time and often can't remember what words he was going to put at the end of a sentence that he is actively speaking.

His money has been hit. He spends a ridiculous amount of money on over-the-counter supplements to feel better.

His house became infested with rodents. Two birds flew into his house one Christmas and had to be professionally removed—, birds that should have been South for the winter. What were they doing at his door?

He breaks pretty much every electronic device he gets into his hands. His garage is a graveyard for laptops that no longer turn on and cell phones with broken screens.

He has wrecked car after car, even though he couldn't get his driving license as a teenager until he took a professional driving course, per his father.

He nearly lost his big toe to a deep gash while at home, doing practically nothing. He lost his glasses and couldn't see without them on a vacation, and his then-wife would not take him to the eye doctor to get new glasses. Reproach is all over him.

He forgets everything. He lives in a harried stressed-out mode, always in a rush and a hurry, but never gets anywhere on time. He makes rushed unfortunate financial decisions often and they lead to losses.

He can't see the most obvious of things. He just can't see it – it's as though he's blindfolded. He walks about and does things that would seem normal to most people. He works, he goes on vacations, but neither he nor his kids *know* if they had a nice time or not on their vacations. I'm not making this up. It takes him (and his kids) over a year, usually two years to know if they had a good time on a previous vacation or not.

He tries to be lighthearted, but he seems miserable.

Not only does he not *believe in* witchcraft, but he would NEVER believe that his only sister is working evil against him. Of course, he tells her ALL of his business. She lives halfway across the country, but she knows ALL of his co-workers, and whatever he knows about these co-workers, including the beautiful but mysteriously dead, young woman.

She is constantly asking the Professional Guy for money. His sister, whom his mother has assigned to take care of -- it is the perfect cover, the perfect set up for this household witch.

Oh, this sister hates her brother's children, so he endeavors to keep them away from each other--, has for years. He could and should have a closer relationship with his kids and is frustrated as to why he doesn't, try as he may. More reproach.

He doesn't believe in witchcraft. My God! Salvation and deliverance prayers would save the professional man's life from reproach, torment, frustration, poverty and from having the rest of his life and relationships with his kids stolen from him.

Now this gets interesting because as Scooby Doo plots go, the sister maybe plotting to get his money for her retirement since she is nearing retirement age now but has nothing, because like a grasshopper, she has never worked consistently.

My concern is that she might be sending incantations to hit the people in *his* life that he likes, admires or loves romantically, but it hits **him** instead of those *people*.

Or, that it is sent to *him*, and the curse may include the **demise of any susceptible romantic interest who is associated with him.**

I kid you not; she's the perpetrator. God showed me, and I know up close and personally because I was *associated* with him. She and I had a nonverbal, states-apart **war**. He was far more susceptible to her witchcraft than I am because GOD.

Thank You, Jesus!

Because of prayer coverage and the Grace of God here I am writing a book that can edify and educate you instead of in a state as the beautiful, young woman who is no longer here --, mysteriously.

So, this professional man has lived his whole life not knowing or realizing that he is **bewitched**, has been bewitched or living a remote-controlled life.

Now, for the first part: What's wrong with me? Applying the Word of God as the standard, I surmised that what might be wrong with **me** is <u>sin</u> which in my case included a dried-up prayer life as I tried to fit it with "regular people." Jesus remedied all that and I endeavor not to sin as much as it is in me and by help of the Holy Spirit. So the sum total is that what is wrong with any of us is sin, disobedience on our part, and household or remote witches in any or all genders.

Evil men, angry men, hurt men are ever calling women *witches*… strange, since these same men say they don't believe in witches or witchcraft and really can't spot one even while being seduced by one. Seriously, don't blame it all on women, there are wizards and warlocks in the world. The devil has too many evil agents.

This Is Not His Real Life

There are no statistics as to whether men or women are more susceptible to witchcraft. We know that no curse can alight without a cause (Proverbs 26:2). We know that the unsaved are open targets, **unfair** game because without God they don't have a chance. That curse will hit – if there is sin, and we have all sinned, without God that curse will alight, it will hit. Period.

The professional man in the previous chapter called himself an Agnostic; he believed in *nothing*. He didn't believe in God; he didn't even believe in the religion that his parents brought him up in, although from the above retelling it is obvious that the culture he grew up in is riddled with witchcraft. Why he didn't know that, why he doesn't know that or couldn't see that may be part of the dulling of the senses. It could be that witchcraft was all around him, so pervasive that he never noticed that what was all around him *was* witchcraft, he only thought it was *normal*.

No, he's not lamenting having lived a bewitched life; he doesn't yet accept that he's bewitched. Of course, I told him. If you haven't met me, I am the type to tell a body something if the Lord gives me release to speak it. So, yes, I told him. He doesn't believe me, and he stays far away from my words. Maybe one day he will realize it. Maybe he won't. Sad, really his entire free will and life has been stolen from him by a jealous, covetous, envious relative with immoral motives.

And this is different than the Old Man interfering in and wrecking my love life all my life, how--?

It's no different. It's evil. The only thing that is different is that I am God's and I have prayers now. I have a prayer covering and my God will contend with those who contend with me. The professional man is professionally Agnostic; he has no one. I feel that at least when he was "associated" with me, there was some Grace for him, but now, unless he is saved now and I don't know it, he has no spiritual protection.

This Is Not Your Life

Ladies may think your own life is the way it is and the way it's supposed to be, but you see men behaving strangely. It's hard to believe that there are "normal" men out here if you never meet one or have never met one. You may have formed a negative opinion of men... you think ungodly things while thinking that those thoughts are *your thoughts,* but they are not.

The death knell is when you start *speaking* what you see in men. This not only draws it to you; it perpetuates it in your life.

Out of the abundance of the heart the mouth speaks. A man (or woman) can have whatsoever he/she says. You start speaking things and they *may* come into manifestation. Careful.

That is exactly what the witches, wizards, the warlocks are doing. If you are speaking ungodly things, you are in their same category now.

If, however you decide to speak what God says over you, your life, your career, your family and relationships then you are walking by faith and using the Godly principle of having whatever you say on the positive side of things.

If you've been bewitched, oppressed by demons, *possessed* – your real life is suppressed and **entities are living another life *through you--*,** through your body and you are not having the opportunity to live your own life. They are having an evil party, living an evil life, using your body and your life for as long as you accept them, allow them, ignore them, or remain powerless to kick them out.

Paul said it is not me that doeth the sin but the sin in him is doing it... it's taken a life of it's own. Or the demons will annoy you, work you, irk you make you anxious until you give in to what they want. It could be a cigarette, it could be ice cream, it could be sex. It is totally out of your character and the you that you believe yourself to be, but there you are doing ungodly things.

Proof is: If you do sinful things and then feel bad, asking yourself, *Why did I do that? It could be that you didn't do it.* If you felt compelled to do a thing, that's *possession*, really, but the bewitchment may make you helpless to defending your will and body from doing the sin act. Possession becomes possible because witchcraft plants an evil seed or sends and evil event into the life of the victim and then the bewitched does the rest of the damage himself.

In the witchcraft victim, thoughts change to evil. Words change to evil. Actions change to evil. This is the perfect environment for a demon or demons.

Don't Accept Them

Have you accepted demons have you consented to them over time, just gotten used to them? Do you now think, *This is the way it is?* Without the Word of God to teach you Truth and the Spirit of God to lead you into all Truth…you won't know jack. All you will know about the "spiritual" is fairytales, leprechauns, witches, goblins, elves, wizards and other things that even though you've been told everything about them, you have been forced to summarize that they are not real – they are make-believe.

There is power in the Word; without the **power** of God and the anointing of His Christ you will be powerless against demonic oppression and possession. Recall, it takes **power** to stop sinning.

When under this heavy, constant witchcraft, this is not even you living your own life. Instead, your **life is being stolen from you**. The joys, the pleasures, the free will that GOD gave you has been stolen by a disembodied spirit (usually more than one: legions) that has no body to conduct a life on Earth, but it still (continually) wants to experience the flesh. So it has chosen **your** flesh to experience "life" through.

You are captive, locked away, helpless like a zombie, walking dead, you are not even living your own life. The demon has traded places in a sense. **It should be locked away,**

but instead, you are. You should be living your life – your best life in Christ. The demon has no desire for Christ, but it wants to experience the flesh life, daily--, 24-7.

That demon is never satisfied, can never be satisfied. How many other human lives do you think it has taken over? You're not the first, but unless it is sent back to the Abyss from where there is no return for early torment, you will not be the last.

Now you know.

Don't Get Used to It

Have you gotten used to other people's demons? Some humans have decided that partying and living it up is THE life they want. It is the way they want to spend their time here on Earth and how they want to use up the precious opportunity they've been given. They choose to waste their life, expend their life, use of the breath of life that God has lent them on futile and temporal things, instead of storing up good treasure in Heaven.

> But lay up for yourselves treasures in heaven, where neither moth nor rust doth corrupt, and where thieves do not break through nor steal: Matthew 6:20

Instead of doing God's express will in the Bible, by the Spirit, they only want to do the will of their flesh. Do you think God sent you to Earth to party and live your carnal flesh life to the max? Let's see. What's happening in Heaven? Is God up in Heaven partying? Are the 24 Elders just doing random stuff? Are beasts around the Throne of God singing pop or R& B music? What the people--, Elders, angels and entities in Heaven are doing is a major clue as to how God conducts Himself. It is a clue as to how the Kingdom of God works, including all that Jesus came to Earth to teach. The parenthetical and prophetic images of Heaven are what Heavenly decorum looks like.

So do you think God sent you to Earth for nothing? Of course, not. Do you think He sent you here with no purpose, no plan? Of course, not. Do you think God sent you here for *whatever*? Do you think God doesn't **know** that you're even here. OF. COURSE. NOT.

Discernment Off

It started as soon as you got here. The fairy tales which are designed to entertain or amuse. The word, *muse* means *a thought* or *to think*. To be a-*mused* means to be without thought. Empty brained. Nobody wants that.

The net effect is to cause you to turn off your discernment. This happens via the person in authority who is caring for you, the hands that are holding you, you trust, should trust or will learn to trust. So whatever they say is gospel to you. No need to look puzzled or second guess it, you've been told, and it must be so. Because I said so whether spoken or not becomes the new order of the day.

God is not a man that He should lie, so because God said so, it is so. But there is no other human or any entity from wicked places or from hell who you should believe just because they said so. There is no one that you should believe just because they are on TV. TV is vetted only for how much money they can make. The internet is the same way. Just because something is in print does not make it true. Search out all things for yourself.

Now that you are all grown up, I give you permission to turn your Discernment BACK ON! Discernment means you have Wisdom, and you know how to use knowledge. Discernment means you use good judgment; you are prudent. Joseph was more prudent than his brothers. It means we are paying attention. We are fully in the moment and aware of what's going on around us. You can hear from God, and you know that you know that you heard from God with confirmation in the Word and in your spirit man.

Having discernment is one thing, but you must USE Discernment. If you are flaky, or wishy-washy and do not MAKE decisions, discernment won't do you much good. Don't be one of those people who says, I should have done such and such. My first mind told me, but I didn't do it. Discernment without proper action is useless.

Practice discernment. There are certain somatic *feels* I get in certain situations. Know yourself. If your head feels different than usual when there is a certain spiritual thing going on, don't quench that feeling. Learn what it goes with. If your stomach feels like butterflies or anxiety, there may be something going on that you need to deal with or you may need to get out of there! Know how your body responds to certain spiritual stimuli and govern yourself accordingly.

I tell you now for your spiritual edification that if I had paid attention to the signs of discernment that God sent me when I was in a dangerous situation and acted accordingly, I would not have gone through a whole bunch of mess that I've gone through in life.

That is what discernment is for.

Doubt and uncertainty can be results of evil witchcraft arrows. Or, it could already be in you from your upbringing. You could be one of those people whose "*No*" was taken away as a kid. At about two years old kids learn, *No* and they assert their will as much as they are allowed to. This is useful later in life. I've read that those whose *No's* are stolen, have their will broken and they often end up as pushovers, drug addicts and or street workers.

Like God, let your Yes be *yes*, and let your No be *No* and let discernment save you from a lot of heartache and heartbreak. Amen.

Unwilling to Recognize a Demon

Fear could be something that you are brought up with in your family, it could be the result of evil arrows. Being unwilling to recognize a demon not so much by sight, but by evil patterns in your life is a problem.

Lots of people think that if it ain't broke don't fix it. So they will even pretend it's not broken so they don't have to look at it or fix it. Something could be fun and ungodly and wrong, but most will think, hey if it's fun; we may, in error accept it. If it's not too bad, we may accept it. If it's not as bad as it used to be we might accept it.

But is it God? Is it of God? Did you specifically ASK God or find it in the Bible?

Recognize God

Not being able to recognize GOD, either His voice or His ways are other ways people get into trouble and stay there.

If a person can't recognize God, then they won't recognize not-God.

Out of Relationship – doing your own thing. Most often, your remote control is the devil's remote control, not your own.

Because without God what power do you have over evil that is sent into your life?

Skin disease – just because that person is your family member doesn't make them Godly, of God or that they mean you a piece of good.

Everyone who says, LORD, LORD will not be saved.

Not everyone who says to Me, 'Lord, Lord,' shall enter the kingdom of heaven, but he who does the will of My Father in heaven.

Matthew 7:21

Over You

I once asked my hair stylist why I couldn't do my hair as well as she could. Her answer was succinct and correct. She said, *"You can't stand over yourself and see the top of your head."*

Wow. I knew instantly that she was on point.

As I work on people's teeth, I too realize that my vantage point is *over* them, so I see everything – the bird's eye view, as they say. If you are never willing to sit still and go, get a haircut you will never have a good cut. If you won't sit in a dental chair and have someone properly clean your teeth or prepare and place a filling, you put yourself at grooming and health disadvantage. Any surgeon that adds, removes or repairs anything on or in your body is standing over you, looking down.

So is our God; He sits high and looks low. He can see it all. God sees it all. But if we are not willing to sit still long enough for Him to tell us things we need to know... **He speaks. He speaks** in many ways. In dreams, in prophetic words, in the Bible, in Rhema words. Sometimes in a song or a movie you can get a message that is important to your life. Out of the mouth of babes, God has even ordained praise.

I recall, even as a pre-teen, I used to say things to my parents, not disrespectfully, but I was sure of what I was saying. They rebuffed my words, but later my words ended up being what they had needed to hear. After they shut me down a few times I stopped sharing things I knew and saw, out of respect for them; but I still knew things.

So we submit to God, else there are things that from our vantage point and from our Grace we will never see or understand... BUT GOD.

Multiple Bewitchments

Why might you be attractive to bewitching? Evil foundation. Evil dedication. Evil altars. Ancestral sin. Personal sin. You've got the magnet that attracts such a curse.

A curse causeless will not alight.

The people you don't have a good feeling about. The people you just don't like. The people you like, but it's obvious that they don't like you. There's a reason for it. Let your discernment kick in. It may be best to stay away from those people. Pray and ask God.

Fake friends, and forced friends are not friends. Change your location, change your friend circle. Pray always. If someone tells you they don't like you, believe them the first time. If someone tells you they are jealous of you, they mean it.

Jealousy is probably the #1 motivator for evil, curses, witchcraft against people--, household witchcraft.

There is environmental witchcraft – there are people who don't even know you who actually hate people in general. They are most likely on assignment (remote control) themselves. People who practice witchcraft have captive souls whether they realize it or not. They believe they are powerful, but what they are doing, what they want to do – the evil they want to do is in line with what the devil wants to do, so the devil empowers them to do their evil. All the while they think they themselves "did this." This is how individuals get drunk with power.

It's Compounding

Maybe you ticked somebody off, irritated some power-struck immature, heathen type person who is bent on vengeance and payback. Perhaps you did nothing at all.

Jilted a girlfriend? Not wise, unless you know what altars she serves at. Rejected a boyfriend? Ditto.

You beat the leading quarterback on the opposing team. His mom or dad could be a whole witch. You won't know until you know. You got the scholarship when that other kid thought he should have gotten it--, we never know what's in an evil heart until we see the evil that comes out of it.

You got the job promotion and the guy who has been there longer than you did not. His wife has a *Jezebel spirit* and what her husband wants, she feels he should get. Tag. You're it. Again.

Someone just saw you and thought you were very beautiful, and they were green with envy. Perhaps you remind them of the girl that stole their high school sweetheart. They don't even know you. It doesn't matter. **Listen to me, it doesn't matter.**

Someone you don't know who doesn't know you is playing around with witchcraft "for fun" and sending out random arrows and for some reason your prayer life has dried up and you have no prayer covering. In that case you could get hit. Tag. Yup. *Again.*

It could be some novice witch or wizard trying to jump into a coven, sending out arrows just for the heck of it. Tag...

You do not know why anyone may have ought against you. But maybe you do. They are angry, but because they are not saved, the *sin not* part doesn't register with them. Or, they are saved, but the are so incensed that the *sin not* part doesn't matter to them.

Any and all these people could want payback. Your ancestors cheated someone in money, a land deal, in business... Your great, great grandmother stole someone else's husband. Of course, it is told as a great, romantic love story but that's not what really happened.

Your great granddad worshipped at strange altars... third and fourth generation stuff is coming. Tag. You're it.

Abraham tithed in Levi; but your evil ancestor sinned IN YOU. You've been tagged. Better pray!

Prayer Covering

This all boils down to: You need a prayer covering. A proper prayer covering requires regular prayers. Daily prayers. We will go deeper later in this book, but as an overview you will use and SAY Prayers of Protection. You should Command the Morning/Command the Day.

You should pray Prayers against witchcraft attack. In the evening pray prayers that Command the Night.

I'm not writing out any of these prayers because you can look them up online, in bookstores, on Youtube there are people already praying them for you. You could join in and pray with those people. The Warfare Prayer Channel on Youtube is one of my channels and I pray all of these types of prayers and many more.

See To It Yourself

God has given you breath. God has set you in dominion. It is said that when the king speaks, heads roll. We move in certain graces the Lord allows. We are kingly as the Lord is King of kings. We are a royal priesthood, so we have authority in spiritual matters, both to minister to others as the Lord directs and allows and also to speak on spiritual matters and to speak, declare and decree against spiritual evil. This is what a king does, he watches over, guards or defends a domain.

See to it yourself.

Oh, and you have a whole throne. At least in your fairy tales don't you remember there was always a king, there was a prince, there was a princess? Notice there was a hierarchy. Also notice there was a witch and or a wizard and that's when the trouble starts. Touché'. Troubles may come but you can put an end to it with prayers and a proper prayer covering.

The days of fairy tales and being read stories has long passed. The days and nights of being lulled to sleep by the voice of another who may or may not be telling you the truth or anything of importance or value to your life are over. The days of wasted breath on entertainment instead of protection are over. You are a king, set in dominion and now you must know that and walk in it.

What domain? Whatever the Lord has given you; ask Him. In the natural it is everything you have stewardship over, houses, cars, family, marriage, children, career, ministry. Don't forget other kingly stuff such as wealth, money, your crown, jewels and anything of value that would diminish the power of your presence in an Earth body. Money is a defense and money is a power.

But before the natural, your battlefield is the in the Spirit. In the Spirit is all those same things as you take care of, protect and speak over those things in the Spirit to protect them first spiritually from the moths, rust, decay and corruption that is trying to move from the spiritual realm into the natural to destroy your purpose, ministry, marriage or life. In the Spirit it is everything spiritual that the LORD has given you, when He gave gifts unto men: spiritual gifts, Fruit of the Spirit: true riches.

Then the Prayers Start

A king speaks and things happen. The Lord is a warrior, and the Lord is His name. If the Lord is a warrior and we are to be like Him, and we are to be in Him and He in us, what do you think we are? Warriors. So we are Kings, priests and warriors. That cannot confuse you because all of us walk in multiple offices in our daily life. We are spouses, brothers, sisters, friends, parents, businessmen and sports enthusiasts when we enter marathons, great chefs when we play opera while making pasta in our own kitchens. We may not be fully expressing each one of these attributes, skills, tasks, or hobbies at the same time, but we are fully gifted and capable to turn on any needed skillset at a moment's notice and be what we need to be to minister in our life. What *office* we are moving in at any given time is evident in how we are ministering at any given time.

Don't say you don't *minister* because you do, all the time. Now, let's minister to the Lord in worship and prayers. Excellent prayers of Protection are the Lord's Prayer. Psalm 91. Psalm 23; they can be found in the Bible in the translation of your choice.

Command the Morning, Command the Day prayers are important. Pray prayers against witchcraft attack. Command the Night

Spiritual warfare for the more serious and advanced prayer warrior as are Courtroom Prayers, Dangerous prayers, Judgmental prayers, Atomic prayers, and Declarations and decrees.

Spiritual warfare for the more serious and advanced prayer warrior as are Fire Prayers, Courtroom Prayers, Dangerous prayers, Judgmental prayers, Atomic prayers, and Declarations and decrees.

Do not fail to command your week, each week. Command your month, each month. Command your seasons, each season. And of course, command your year.

If the problem is humbling yourself before God and you won't do that, you've got an anti-Christ problem. No I didn't say that you are the anti-Christ, but the *spirit of anti-Christ* is on the throne of your heart, if you won't acknowledge God and humble yourself before Him at all and especially in prayer. Where you should have enthroned the Lord Jesus Christ there is a whole demon perched there.

For many what you just read is the knowledge you need to knock that evil spirit (demon) off that a throne that you should be working to your full advantage, spiritually speaking. And *speaking* is what you should be doing.

What Kind of King?

What kind of king sits on a throne and does nothing, says nothing? People and God may be looking at you are thinking, *He's a king, he's got a throne and a domain but he's not making any decrees; he's not **saying** anything.*

A king who says nothing is puppet king. A mannequin, a marionette. If you don't have control of your own strings, **someone will take control of them.** You may not be a very aggressive person but please know that some people and all kinds of evil are looking for power. In so doing, they look for a void of leadership or for any weakness. That is, when it appears that a person who should have authority is not taking authority, not using or exerting power (leadership) in a certain area a potential usurper will try to take over and take that position. This is evident at work, in business when the quiet, mousy type is doing a great job and saying nothing, while the loudmouth who isn't doing much at all tries to take credit for the work that's been done in order to get the promotion.

Sadly it happens in real life more than in the movies.

That happens in the spirit too. Uh huh.

From birth the training you get from the fairytales is that all the spiritual stuff that *is real* is **not** real therefore you don't have anything to do when you grow up. Just grow up and loaf around like a grasshopper instead of a king is the programming. A spiritual assault comes to your domain (your world) and you're the king, but you've been programmed to think that nothing has happened. You're programmed to think that only the illiterate and ignorant think that spiritual things, or that invisible things are real.

You do nothing, you say nothing. That's as good as Evil wants it. *Looky there,* they may say, *There's another king who doesn't know he's a king. Look at all he's got; look at all God has given him and he's doing NOTHING with it. Let's go get it.*

Of course their first goal is to redirect you, derail you, keep you from getting what you should be getting—as soon as possible. First part of the strategy is to teach you that they are not real. Fairytales cloak enemies that should be visible to you, even though they are invisible, you could have been taught to see them spiritually or at least by discernment sense either their presence or the results of their actions against you (and others).

But life has you behaving as a lackluster do-nothing king who won't even protect your own domain. You look either like the most ignorant king ever, or, the laziest...oh please, will you at least remove the lint from your navel and scrub the toe jam from your feet?

I'm sharing this from my own experience. I was going through the fairytale version of my life where I had believed the things I *liked* form the fairy tales and thought life worked like that. Oh, the secular, pop music and movies on love affairs and romance – none of that stuff is how real love and relationships work. It was idolatry to believe any song, whether it was beautiful or had great lyrics, a good beat, or whether my friends liked the song because it was number one on the Billboards. Who is this

Bill guy anyway? The music of our lives should be songs and psalms that say and echo what God says our lives should be. Are any of the people who write secular music other than secular? Are they saved? Are they walking in Salvation or selling music?

So there I was in the early years of my "saved" life thinking Salvation was just an event and then I could do whatever else I wanted and still have insurance against hell's fires. **That's NOT how Salvation works. That is not what God intends.**

I confess this all because my prayer life was either dry or minimal, and I do not want that for you. *Now I lay me down to sleep* and an occasional grace over a meal if people were present is NOT a prayer life and does not make a prayer covering. In addition, the peer pressure of doing what everyone else is doing leads to sin; it is the broad way. And either in my sin and/or because of ancestral sin curses that were sent my way *hit*.

God is great and God is gracious; I do feel that in His Mercy God did not allow things to be as bad as they could be, but the trajectory of my life, the level of my comfort, the glory of my star has diminished or dimmed intermittently over my life. That doesn't mean that I haven't rebounded and recovered, **in Christ.** But the work and the discomfort that evil disorder sends and requires for remedy can be exhausting unless your spirit man is willing and strong. It is so much easier to avoid all these mistakes.

Pay attention to the words in this book, they are to help you and edify you. As bad as evil is, as bad as evil human agents are, God will avenge all disobedience in your obedience.

You keep yourself in order under the Mighty Hand of God and the fiery darts of the enemy won't strike you!

Pray, *little k*, king: PRAY!

Thank you for reading this book. You can hear more teachings on like subjects on the Dr. Miles Youtube Channel.

Christian books by this author:

AK: Adventures of the Agape Kid

AMONG SOME THIEVES

As My Soul Prospers

Behave

Blindsided: *Has the Old Man Bewitched You?*

Churchzilla (The Wanna-Be Bride of Christ)

The Coco-So-So Correct Show

Demons Hate Questions

Do Not Orphan Your Seed

Do Not Work for Money

Don't Refuse Me Lord

The FAT Demons

got Money?

Let Me Have a Dollar's Worth

Living for the NOW of God

Lord, Help My Debt

Lose My Location

Made Perfect In Love

The Man Safari *(Really, I'm Just Looking)*

Marriage Ed., *Rules of Engagement & Marriage*

My Life As A Slave

Name Your Seed

Plantation Souls

The Poor Attitudes of Money

Power Money: Nine Times the Tithe

The Power of Wealth

Seasons of Grief

Seasons of War

The *spirit* of Poverty

The Throne of Grace, *Courtroom Prayers*

The Unseen Life (deep)

This Old Man (forthcoming)

Warfare Prayer Against Poverty

When the Devourer is Rebuked

The Wilderness Romance

Other Journals & Devotionals by this author:

The Cool of the Day – Journal for times spent with God

got HEALING? Verses for Life

got HOPE? Verses for Life

got WISDOM? Verses for Life

got GRACE? Verses for Life

got JOY? Verses for Life

got PEACE? Verses for Life

got LOVE? Verses for Life

He Hears Us, Prayer Journal *in 4 different colors*

I Have A Star, Dream Journal *in styles for kids, teen, young adult and up.*

I Have A Star, Guided Prayer Journal, *2 styles: Boy/ Girl*

J'ai une Etoile, Journal des Reves

Let Her Dream, Dream Journal *in multiple colors*

Men Shall Dream, Dream Journal, *(blue or black)*

My Favorite Prayers (in 4 styles)

My Sowing Journal (in three different colors)

Tengo una Estrella, Diario de Sueños

Wise Counsel Journal

Illustrated children's books by this author:

Big Dog (8-book series)

Do Not Say That to Me

Every Apple

Fluff the Clouds

I Love You All Over the World

Imma Dance

The Jump Rope

Kiss the Sun

The Masked Man

Not During a Pandemic

Push the Wind

Tangled Taffy

What If?

Wiggle, Wiggle; Giggle, Giggle

Worry About Yourself

You Did Not Say Goodbye to Me

www.ingramcontent.com/pod-product-compliance
Lightning Source LLC
Chambersburg PA
CBHW070852050426
42453CB00012B/2165